Weather

THE

POETRY
SERIES

Weather

POEMS BY DAVE LUCAS

The University of Georgia Press
Athens & London

Published by The University of Georgia Press
Athens, Georgia 30602
www.ugapress.org
© 2011 by Dave Lucas
All rights reserved
Set in 10.5/15 Minion Pro
Printed and bound by Thomson-Shore

The paper in this book meets the guidelines for
permanence and durability of the Committee on
Production Guidelines for Book Longevity of the
Council on Library Resources.

Printed in the United States of America

15   14   13   12   11   P   5   4   3   2   1

Library of Congress Cataloging-in-Publication Data

Lucas, Dave, 1980–
Weather : poems / by Dave Lucas.
        p.   cm. — (The VQR poetry series)
Includes bibliographical references.
ISBN-13: 978-0-8203-3882-8 (pbk. : alk. paper)
ISBN-10: 0-8203-3882-6 (pbk. : alk. paper)
I. Title.
PS3612.U236W43 2011
811'.6 — dc22   2010044222

British Library Cataloging-in-Publication Data available

For my mother

In memory of my father

for always night and day
I hear lake water lapping with low sounds by the shore

—WILLIAM BUTLER YEATS

the gods grow out of the weather

—WALLACE STEVENS

Contents

Acknowledgments

Thanks to the editors of the following publications, in which some of the poems in this collection first appeared, sometimes in slightly different form:

American Poetry Review: "Firefly," "The Twenty-first Century"

Field: "On a Portrait by Lucian Freud"

Little Star: "Lunar Calendar," "The New Poetry"

The Nation: "Beach Pea"

Paris Review: "Lexicon," "To Alyce, on Her Engagement"

Pleiades: "Self-Portrait"

Poetry: "Lines for Winter," "Suburban Pastoral"

Poetry Northwest: "Of the Tragedies"

River Styx: "After Love," "Lake Erie Monster"

Shenandoah: "November," "'They Wonder at the Star'"

Slate: "Steelhead"

The Sun: "The Dog, in the Presence of Wolves," "For Madeleine, in Another June"

Threepenny Review: "Epithalamium," "Midwestern Cities," "Orpheus, Aside," "Red-tailed Hawk," "To Say Nothing"

The Virginia Quarterly Review: "All Souls Night," "At the Cuyahoga Flats," "The Fox," "Lives of the Saints"

"December 1678, New France" was printed by the 92nd Street Y and the Unterberg Poetry Center in a pamphlet for the 2005 "Discovery"/*The Nation* reading. "Epithalamium" was reprinted in *Best New Poets 2005*, edited by George Garrett and Jeb Livingood (Samovar Press). "November" was reprinted in *Poetry: An Introduction* (Bedford/St. Martin's, 6th ed., 2009) and in *The Bedford Introduction to Literature* (Bedford/St. Martin's, 9th ed., 2010), both edited by Michael Meyer.

I would like to thank the University of Virginia for its Henry Hoyns Fellowship, during which many of these poems were written, as well as the Sewanee Writers' Conference for its Tennessee Williams Scholarship, the Bread Loaf Writers' Conference for its Carol Houck Smith Scholarship, and the Unterberg Poetry Center and *The Nation* for their "Discovery"/*The Nation* Prize.

Thanks to all at the University of Georgia Press who helped these poems become a book, and in particular Jon Davies, Regan Huff, Jane Kobres, John McLeod, Erin Kirk New, and Beth Snead.

For the support, suggestions, patience and friendship that made this volume possible, I am grateful to Sarah Barber, Jeff Brannon, Laurie and John Casteen, Danielle Chapman and Christian Wiman, Michael Collier, Martha Collins, Roger Craik, Mike Croley, Brad Dougherty, Beth Ann Fennelly, Ryan Fox, Melissa and Blake Frei, Mike Gali, Ted Genoways, Ed Hirsch, Mark Jarman, Ann Kjellberg, Wendy Lesser, John McBratney, Maureen McHugh, Phil Metres, Maryclaire Moroney, Tony Morris, Jason Nemec, Tom Nevin, Richard Newman, Meghan O'Rourke, Gregory Orr, Lynn Powell, Lisa Russ Spaar, Arin and Joe Tait, and Shannon Thomas, as well as to the memory of Craig Arnold.

To Alan Shapiro, Dave Smith, and Mark Strand.

And especially to my mentors, Ellen Geisler, George Bilgere, Rita Dove, and Charles Wright.

Finally, to my family, and to Amy.

Weather

Midst of a Burning Fiery Furnace

Let the foundries burn the whole city then.
Black the edges and the brazen joints.
Let the salamander sleep in his well of flame.
Because the worst has happened, and yet
so much more remains to be burnt,
smelt and milled and cast. These remains.
Suppose this blistered city would smolder
well after all those who live by the blast
of the furnace have left themselves to ash.
I have heard of that alchemy of steel—
I am familiar with the dying arts. Let them burn
the dark night livid, my poor republic
of ingot and slag. I am also seething
in my depths, I too have come to forge.

Beach Pea

Leave beauty to the rose
and its lexicon of crimsons.
O ruby petal and holy thorn—
poets, you can have it.

You, beach pea, rooted
in sand when all this land
was lake, when this lake
was Atlantic coast,

stranded when the glaciers
calved and receded—
leaving you and sea rocket,
purple sand-grass and spurge.

What genuine science,
what skill in your flowering:
you conjure nitrogen
from thin air and hold it,

hard as November wind,
in your roots. Deep
in the sterile loam, they spread
and keep what water they can.

Hardscrabble, this scratch
of beach offers nothing
but swells of dry surf,
break and wash of waves

like the back and forth
of xylem and phloem
in your thin frame's
tiny musculature.

Pastel and crepe petal,
flower of work and mettle,
spread out, spread deep.
Bow to no one, to no rose.

Steelhead

Morning spreads the lake
still, solemn; breath
hangs like an insult
in the steely chill. But
not a word

for hours now, just rock
and sweep of Erie seiche.
The line vibrates in the wind,
tuned *pianissimo*. Then
a hit—

jolt—fish on—the sudden
taut line, the familiar
struggle and thresh, slap
of water, fish out of water,
flapping, its flesh

a kaleidoscope of lake and light.
It falls back, and runs,
the reel zipping out more line
with each flick of dorsal
and caudal.

If we could see the eyes
or the blunt spade
of its head, we might claim
to see courage in them,
or spirit.

But what propels its
ten slick pounds
through the water is beyond
what we know of ourselves,
beyond

the education of the angler,
who lets out the line, then
pulls back, falconer tethering
unmanned hawk, until
the moment

when he jerks back,
when the water gives up
its silver cache.
And then the hollow drum
of fish

on boat. Now we can see
the black eyes, the snub
nose and gunmetal scale,
the prehistoric fins
that keep on

treading phantom water.
The gills gape. The fish flips
itself over once, and stares
back with what must be called
defiance.

Red-tailed Hawk

The cool reconnaissance
of the cursive *m*,
gone lethal: sheered

earthward, the brown
and scarlet slash of wing
and tail tempt the eye,

but how, if one could
catch an instant's glimpse,
the black talons

would gleam, how visceral
as they pierce the body.
The vole rushing

on ecstatic instinct
is caught in engineering
beyond its rodent brain,

though one wonders
if any mind comprehends
the horrific yank back

skyward, the slam
of immediate updraft.
Distance dulls hawk

into idea, once more
a subtle brushstroke
on the blue. Soon

all belongs to the mind—
predator and prey,
the brief, shrill screech,

the thatch of nest
in some tall pine, and chicks
just waking to their hunger.

Firefly

In summer, when the bullfrogs open
their elastic throats to song
and dusk purples the sallow field,
they appear:
                        their first blink
is as winter's last fleck of snow.

Even those the boys (in their Freudian rage)
have swatted die in a tiny halo,
the naked bulb of the abdomen.

Soon the earth is constellated with flies
—satellites in a sex-struck orbit—
beaconing to the wingless females below.

It is as we have imagined in our ecstasies.
The body is filled with light.

Lake Erie Monster

Brontosaur, behemoth,
                    skiff-wrecker, mammoth—
your brutal kith and kin
                    are those only imagined
into the lacustrine
                    fresh depths: Champlain,
Okanagan, and Ness;
                    a family to obsess
so many would-be Ahabs
                    in cryptozoology labs.
We who must believe
                    are achingly naive
or deeply paranoid.
                    Rumor, bunk, tabloid,
and money-flushing dives
                    dredge water from the waves
and little else. Why, then,
                    would-be leviathan,
do we insist on you?
                    Of all that we pursue,
from bleeding amaranth
                    to cuirassed coelacanth,
what's saved from mystery
                    is doomed to history,
from the shade of nature
                    to Latin nomenclature.
More than analogy
                    and book biology,
a thing that is, and is
                    all *sui generis*—
never be so lured
                    from the water where you're moored.

Swim, loom aloof
                    from any hint of proof.
When the ore ships freight
                    their cargo through the night
and Arctic winds blow
                    across the lake's white brow,
let us doubt your fluke,
                    the waters that crest and break
and crush against the bulwark.
                    Hulk, reign, lurk.

To the Lake

If it lack ocean's ageless profundity
—the spirit moving on the face of its waters,
its grand mythology of saints and martyrs—
if it is bound, but not the boundary,
let it be so. If failing industry
has cast its cupfuls mineral and bitter,
still hesitate, Erie's sons and daughters,
to call it secondary to the sea.
For every winter with its skull-matte glaze
of surface ice, recall that, deep beneath,
swim fossil sturgeon, walleye, muskellunge,
safe as a rapier nested in its sheath.
As winter holds fast, may you hold your tongue
until May waters warm it into praise.

December 1678, New France

... the universe does not afford its parallel.

—FATHER LOUIS HENNEPIN

Hours away, the glacial crescendo began,
beginning in the gut—the heavy rhythm
of men's steps after days of walking—
so that we all might have assumed
a spell of frost-bitten madness.
All the mastlike pines, though rooted
in the frozen earth, swayed as if in stress
of a storm at sea, relentlessness of only water.
With an instant not one of us can recollect
it was in our ears like the sea in a conch.
We trouped on toward the muted roar.
I cannot know how much time passed
or if each man bore, as I did, such a weight
of zealous thirst and the sour taste of fear,
as if the Day of Judgment dawned
in some clearing up ahead, beyond our sight.
A veil of mist, mist like felt, fell on our brows
before, at last, we came to the place where
indeed the trees gave way to clearing. Beyond
a smallish ridge of sharpened rock
we saw the great author of that deafening:
a wall of water that seemed to flow
neither up nor down, but to hang, a tapestry
of such wonder to put even the unbeliever
on his knees. Its punished rock is obscured,
where it falls, by clouds of fog that rival
the huge curtains of flume blowing above.
Rocks of indescribable size—houses, cities

of rock lie beneath its brutal wave.
Everywhere the water is white, whiter
than the crests of waves in winter storms.
The tallest trees around are as men
in the shadow of titans. The exactitude
of the Lord's creation—what scale,
what grandeur and love for beauty.
What marvelous capacity for surprise.
In this, he reveals to us apocalypse,
with calm before and after. How soon
the river reasserts its peace, and flows
from such violence into such accord.
I dreamed that night of Our Lord walking
over the great cascade, and the astonished,
the unbelieving looking on—do not doubt
but on that Day, when the wood of this life
breaks into glorious clearing, these waters
will fall as monument and rise into the air
with celestial grace.—In the morning
we broke camp and set out toward
Lake Erie, to the west. Again, for hours,
it poured its endless, furious syllable.
We heard it in our heads for weeks.

At the Cuyahoga Flats

Here, in the river's oxbow-bend and silt,
the muddy unmarked grave of Republic Steel.
Here is the elegy to ore and pellet:
inertial loaders, the quiet of the mill.

See how deliberate the passing barge—
as if somewhere hotter furnaces are lit.
Rust in the water and reclining drawbridge:
oxide and spall, the color of ash at sunset.

River on Fire

Stranger, the way of the world is crooked,
and anything can burn. Nothing impossible.
Who comes to send fire upon the earth may find
as much already kindled, may find his city
bistre and sulfurous. Pitched and grimed.
On those suffered banks we sat down and wept.
There the prophets, if there had been prophets,
would have baptized us in fire. Who says impossible
they fill his mouth with ash, they quench him
as if a man could be made steel. A crooked way
the world wends, and the rivers, and the prophets.
Go down and tell them what you have seen:
that the river burned and was not consumed.

Hulett Ore Unloaders

> Beginning in earnest today, [crews will] dismantle
> the Hulett ore unloaders, those huge, rusting, ancient
> machines on Cleveland's lakefront that for decades
> scooped ore from the bellies of freighters.
> —*Cleveland Plain Dealer*, 31 January 2000

Unfinished cathedrals buttressed against themselves
or lakeshore sentinels or the cantilevered ribcage
of some dread unimagined mastodon, or anything
but simply disassembled and warehoused, obsolete
as the locked-up words in forgotten hoards,
that bold, consonantal tribal clang—
or the dead tongue with which we bless the dead.

Midwestern Cities

You Midwestern cities, you threadbare capitals,
lost satellites, will your outskirts never end?
Will your suburbs run each other through
and your accents bleed into a slang of silk and husk?
Dawn is slipping across the chain-smoking factories
of Pittsburgh and Cleveland, where the third shift
sleeps off its Yuengling, where pierogi boil and stanch.
Wake, Detroit, the morning molts over 10 Mile.
Rise, parched Indianapolis; rise, great skyscraping
Chicago, the odors of your millions soap the El.
Cincinnati, St. Louis, Milwaukee, Minneapolis,
your waters run on. Your congregations hymn,
the billboards declare *The Second Coming
could come at any second*. From anywhere,
Akron or Grand Rapids. From Gary, Kenosha, Duluth.

"They Wonder at the Star"

Frost-scored, ache-early
hibernal small hours:
my father lifts me awake,
blankets and mittens me.

The lake lay in its black
glass sheet and shelf.
My father's coffee seethes.
He angles the telescope.

Its metal cold-cuffs
my eye. Tunnel and void,
the stars shiver against
my trembling cheeks.

Hours we wait. No star,
no omen. Nothing in so much
nothing. Dawn stirs
like blood before a blush.

Comet, your pale hawk
and haze defied me then,
centurial phoenix,
nebulous *Dutchman*.

A father's father ago,
this earth passed through
the ice-bright cloud
of your gaseous coma,

though I doubt they craned
their necks from the fields,
skyward, toward the sailor-
blessed red of dusk.

But I know your shape,
sabre-star: you hang above
the Damoclean English
before Hastings, heralding

the Gallic smoothing
of the old rough tongue.
Isti mirant stella,
but I am filled less

with wonder than this
thawing indignation.
By your return, I will
have buried my father;

my life will arc toward
its own end. Arrive
again in the predawn dark
with your illustrious

dust trail, millennia of ice.
I will not rise from sleep for you.
Come gloried in color.
I will not be moved.

The Rain Again

For who could stop it,
could more than marvel as these slivers
slash flush across the spheres.
As ozone shivers and the oaks split.
No wonder the most awful gods
live there, cruel squalls in those clouds.
The earth must be a saint, I think,
to suffer so. To wait for the rivers
to pour themselves out. Small comfort it is
that the world is old, and mostly water.

Wires

for George Bilgere

Birds perch there, flutter, stretch, then fly,
as if the wires had given consent.
As if they could surround the earth,
wires travel on, past every bend.

Branches will break. But wires bend
and sag, like us: worked hard since birth.
The estate bequeathed by every parent:
the heartache of an endless sky.

The Children

The harvest of children has already begun.
That infant scent is nowhere on their skin.
How grotesquely long their arms and legs,
their pustulant foreheads sick with grease.
Hair bursts forth upon their lineless faces.

Sophomores

They are the zealots of June.
Off now into summer's scald and thrill—
the extravagant boys and their boasts;
and the beautiful girls, quiet and apart,
as if their beauty were an inconsolable grief.
In its thrall, in the gut of that sluttish beast,
they are grist for its mortar and mill.
The rapture of the sun, of every endless
blood-fused night, shall coin and mint them new.
They laugh at autumn, spare no thought
for the death rattle in the leaves. They believe
that summer would vuln herself to feed them.
We would pity them, if pity is the word
for having washed here, on this strange shore.
The stars, from here, seem cold,
though they burn like nothing we can know.

For Madeleine, in Another June

I was wrong, a day came
when I didn't think of you.
Summer passed over like an immense bird.
Another garish Fourth,
August with its sleepless heat,
both of us less
and less sorry. An air conditioner
hummed through the day's work.

Suburban Pastoral

Twilight folds over houses on our street;
its hazy gold is gilding our front lawns,
delineating asphalt and concrete
driveways with shadows. Evening is coming on,
quietly, like a second drink, the beers
men hold while rising from their plastic chairs
to stand above their sprinklers, and approve.

Soon the fireflies will rise in lucent droves—
for now, however, everything seems content
to settle into archetypal grooves:
the toddler's portraits chalked out on cement,
mothers in windows, finishing the dishes.
Chuck Connelly's cigarette has burned to ashes;
he talks politics to Roger in the drive.

"It's all someone can do just to survive,"
he says, and nods—both nod—and pops another
beer from the cooler. "No rain. Would you believe—"
says Chuck, checking the paper for the weather.
At least a man can keep his yard in shape.
Somewhere beyond this plotted cityscape
their sons drive back and forth in borrowed cars:

how small their city seems now, and how far
away they feel from last year, when they rode
their bikes to other neighborhoods, to score
a smoke or cop a feel in some girl's bed.
They tune the radio to this summer's song
and cruise into the yet-to-exhale lung
of August night. Nothing to do but this.

These are the times they'd never dream they'll miss—
the hour spent chasing a party long burned out,
graphic imagined intercourse with Denise.
This is all they can even think about,
and thankfully, since what good would it do
to choke on madeleines of *temps perdu*
when so much time is set aside for that?

Not that their fathers weaken with regret
as nighttime settles in—no, their wives
are on the phone, the cooler has Labatt
to spare; at ten the Giants play the Braves.
There may be something to romanticize
about their own first cars, the truths and lies
they told their friends about some summer fling,

but what good is it now, when anything
recalled is two parts true and one part false?
When no one can remember just who sang
that song that everybody loved? What else?
It doesn't come to mind. The sprinkler spits
in metronome; they're out of cigarettes.
Roger folds up his chair, calls it a day.

The stars come out in cosmic disarray,
and windows flash with television blues.
The husbands come to bed, nothing to say
but *'night.* Two hours late—with some excuse—
their sons come home, too full of songs and girls
to notice dew perfect its muted pearls
or countless crickets singing for a mate.

After Love

The day's stories staling in the mouth.
The task of folding down the collar over the tie.
The foreignness of the lamp on the opposite nightstand.
The useless toothbrush in its slot.
The darknesses in the rooms one enters.
The old sweater with its runs and knots, each a lump in the throat.
The smell of nothing cooking.

To Alyce, on Her Engagement

Quiet, my tiny violins, salve
the poor chests beaten bruise-grey with grief.
May you always be so happy that it stings me.

Epithalamium

After they each had landed in divorce,
my parents met each other in a bar—
the Robin Hood, off Euclid. Unpopular
and dark (the teachers' after-school resource),
just right for a mutual friend to introduce
David and Barb. A Chardonnay, a beer.
A smile and laugh. I am that second's scar.
Next August they were married, on a course
to Dad's dominion of the couch and grill,
Mom in the kitchen, separate and severe.
So strange to envy this, their singling of plurals:
the drowsy, boring breaking of the fever
I burn with, as I wait in bars for girls
I may or may not care about forever.

It Will Be Rain Tonight

for Amy

I am eating well, my love,
I have poured wine with my meal
while the candles lick and wane.
I have set out plate on plate of fruit,
I am seeing to my guests.

I am sleeping sound, my love,
I am no longer counting
phases of the insomniac moon.
I make no promises in the dark.
I have left that sad city blinking behind.

I have set the past adrift, my love,
I have stood on the bank
while the barge burned to ash and dirge.
I have left only crumbs behind me,
I have sown my fields with salt.

I have hardened my heart, my love,
I offer no quarter or relief
despite all manner of plagues.
I have turned away from miracles,
I have turned, my love, into the rain.

You Asked What the Heart Can Carry

                        I said stones,
a sack of shards and earth

to sag the trusses, splay joint and hip.
In weather such as this,

the pines blown bald
and shagged with snow. Through darks,

amnesiac stigmatic dark
our mothers never dreamed to fear for us.

I said stones. You asked how long.
I said until the sand they come to.

To Say Nothing

That was blackberry season, passed
in a glance, and our iodine fingertips.

That music, one feted autumn:
one glutted month of oysters' grit and quartz.

How the leaves drowned in gapes of air,
how little we cared for them

or for the melody bending across staves—
all the lovely songbirds bound elsewhere.

To say nothing of winter. To touch
summer only as a blush touched

your skin, faintly. That music, once,
and again in florid spring. Once I thought

all things had been planned for me.
Not this room, love, not this unsteady violin.

On a Portrait by Lucian Freud

for Rita Dove

Must it end like this? Desire
in his beat-up oxfords and grey trousers
smarms off, does not look back.
Thus this boredom,
the body's naked own: same pie-crust flesh,
ripple of breast, pudendal curl.

Must the sofa unravel this way?
That the head finds a pillow
in the soft crook of arm
is no surprise, nor the ankle
blanketed with curdled thigh.
But must the light be so harsh in the room?
Must the footsteps?

A Sudden Gust of Wind

And the pages paper everywhere
in flights of blank birds. All out of order.
All's out of order but the hilarious wind.

Lives of the Saints

In all the paintings
they share the look of impatience,
as if embarrassed by the rich oils, the stretched canvas
in which their gaze is caught, down to the pupil.
Here, among the attributes of lion and wolf,
the transverse cross, they suffer the interminable
tyranny of this world, their eyes turned
histrionically upward. This place,
not the body barbed with arrows, is the martyrdom.
The tallow burns low toward kingdom come.

We have asked their intercession,
not their pity. This is why we turn
to portraiture and still life, where the bottle remains
unemptied, the zest of an orange
trails tenuously, but holds. Our absence
is of no consequence to them. They have no taste
for bread alone, and no ear
for the songs that make us weep in hurt and joy.

Orpheus, Aside

Soon I shall be old.
My limbs will root themselves
and my eyes will milk over.
When I speak, my voice
will vulture and scrap.
Even the animals
tire of this gypsy sorrow,
and the rocks, and the leaves.
And the dead stay dead.

There is nothing to say,
as much to sing.
O how I have sung
to the gods of silence
in their own tongue—.
Nothing changes:
the dead stay dead,
the rocks are not moved
even a single inch,
the rivers will not stop
rushing toward the sea.

The Fox

for Ryan

Because the hunted learn a furtive grace
that hunters never know: pursued, escape
becomes an art of need, as serfs took tripe
discarded from the master's table-place

and founded *haute cuisine*. And so, the hounded
fox, hidden two dogs deep in earth, may perk
and snarl, may offer a triumphant bark.
The thwarted dogs yelp away, confounded.

The Barber

for Sarah

Not merely the attendant
of beards, trimmed hair, and chair-bound
stubble-razing—more, as in
the medieval minting
of the word, when drying rags
incarnadined the white poles.
Let blood, split hairs, pulled teeth, trays
of carious leeches (*leech*,
from Old High German, leaves us
physician) limn science and
superstition, exegetes
of belief. What's inside must
be brought out.

No quondam occupation,
this—ask Figaro, he of
the barber arias, whose
skill is not only tonal
razoring, whose song is bled
out like humors, the cold blade
brandished, stropped.

In Appalachia

for M. C.

Something you said
about mountains once,
and valleys, what happens
to language in their lees.
No, what happens beneath
their weight, in shafts
where stone sheds stone,
where men come up
from that mineral cell
and say nothing
they need not say.

What happens first
is earth. Ore-smelt cools
and plate shunts plate.
Splints the compound
fracture of ground
where none yet walked.
A scar of mountains:
generations of trees
then, before us, before
the first flit of a bird
in the smoke-dark leaf.

What happens. Fits of life
here settle, the earth
scried and striated.
They wield and build,
choke on the earth
that chalks them up.
As you said once, of
mountains. Something
you said about what happens:
people shut up
in houses of a tongue.

Letter to a Friend

for J. N.

Here are the boy kings in our shabby suits.
Every autumn morning now more our fathers,
and they more similar to theirs, asleep
within the sides of hills, in their old clothes.
Every stiff drink we toasted to ourselves,
promised the promises no lover keeps,
forever and the sea. What we believed
was owed us belonged, instead, to the world.
The girls we loved let down their milk to sons.
This is the life we swore our oaths against,
of compromise and failure. Leave it be.
For here we stand where exiles turn their backs—
if that seems too grand, consider the city
we leave behind, where none build but build towers.
Let us go singing, friend, toward that distance
where all is ruins. Do the broken not make music?
Sing ruin then. Sing ruin that it be sweet.

Dream after News of the Poet's Death

All at once they come the saints in agony the horses of the sea

swift stagger of hooves the horses unbroken saints uncorrupted

We Who Keep the Mystery

for Ellen Geisler

Though it is dark now,
in the arch cathedrals of the world
and in its ramshackle churches
the prayers of the faithful and of doubters alike
dissolve among themselves and whisper
back and forth to each other
like the sound of unread pages
in an empty house. You cannot hear them,
sleeping as you are, but perhaps
you have started from a dream sometime
to hear the house gently creak in a sighing wind
or spent a long night awake and worried
over both the living and the dead
as our lady who listens closely and weeps
while her son hangs there on his cross
where it is dark now, and quiet.

The Dog, in the Presence of Wolves

How fallen from them, their blood-matted fur,
eyes urine-yellow and live with knowledge.
Your body slackened, post-fang, post-sinew;
how dull the arrowed bulb of your nose. All day
you have stalked and wagged around the yard.
After our meal, its quieted clatter, the house glows
against the deepening sky. The trees disappear
into the woods. Out there whiskers pluck
to danger, hungry mouths begin to wet.
What light the tamed moon has kept for itself
glistens on the pack's withers, their roan pelts,
the terrible claws. The sleep of a home
is forgetful sleep: when, from across miles
of wood and soil, they quest their howl,
you perk your sudden ears as if to comprehend
a language turned to gibberish, irreconcilable.
Though in your dreams you bay and twitch, you feast.

Equinox and After

Now the rake-scratch and cull of yellowed leaves,
the missile acorns and the squirrel's canter,
tulip-cigars that prophesy hard winter.
The sugar maples conflagrate above.

Pagan Halloween mounts its corn-husk throne.
The thigh-thick gourd and apple, fattened to harvest,
the urgent geese now on their southern thrust,
the daylight steeped to darkness whisper *soon*.

November

October's brief, bright gush is over.
Leaf-lisp and fetch, their cold-tea smell
raked to the curb in copper- and shale-
stained piles, or the struck-match sweet of sulfur

becoming smoke. The overcast
sky the same slight ambergris.
Hung across it, aghast surprise
of so many clotted, orphaned nests.

All Souls Night

Autumn and its thousand adjectives have come
to this, a swither in the trees,
their limbs bronchial and backlit in the gloam.
The groundhog drowses toward his long sleep.
And I am occupied with the dead, whose night
this is, to whom every night belongs.
The earth hoards them in a miserly embrace,
and we sit by our fires or blinking lamps and try
to recall the husk of a voice, the fallow scent
of grandfathers. Tonight they search the earth,
it is said, wandering as strangers to houses
they no longer recognize. Supper waits
on the table, with immaculate patience.
Perhaps it is true—they follow what sounded
like a familiar voice, a face they think
they might have known, stilled in sleep.
The crust of frost the morning brings may prove
it true, a heave in the land, as last confessions
whispered to the soil which holds them, holds
the bulbs we planted for the spring, and hope for.
The earth will sleep now for its season, the earth
to which, known and unknown, all flesh shall come.

Lines for Winter

Poor muse, north wind, or any god
who blusters dusk-bleak across the lake
and sows the earth earth-deep with ice.
A hoar of fur stung across the vines:
here the leaves in full flush, here
abandoned to four and farther winds.
Bless us, any god who crabs the apples
and seeds the leaf and needle evergreen.
What whispered catastrophe, winter.
What a long night, beyond the lamplight,
the windows and the frost-ferned glass.
Bless the traveler and the hearth he travels to.
Bless our rough hands, wind-scabbed lips,
bless this our miscreant psalm.

Lunar Calendar

WOLF MOON

The snow spreads like an opened hand,
like their bay echoing over the rime fields.

HUNGER MOON

A night without sleep: stars wheel the sky.
An empty stomach is February cold.

WORM MOON

The earth softens, a forgiving heart.
The earthworm emerges, and the robin soon.

PINK MOON

Moss pink, ground phlox. A rose
by any name could not be sweeter.

HARE MOON

Now the flowers in full unison,
now the hare like light across their petals.

STRAWBERRY MOON

The berry's sweet, short season:
gather ye flowers, and so and so.

BUCK MOON

His antlers push through, velvet and bone.
All majesty is birthed in pain.

STURGEON MOON

In haze and halo, by its reddish hint
let our lines snap tight, grow heavy.

HARVEST MOON

Late lantern, and by its light a glut:
beans, rice, corn, pumpkin, squash.

HUNTER'S MOON

The leaves fall and fallen, the deer fattened.
The cold causes the arrow to sing.

BEAVER MOON

Now set the traps. We will shiver for furs
before the swamps sparkle over with cold.

LONG NIGHT'S MOON

Skeletal, sclerotic moon, pendulum standing
winter still. We shall sleep you away.

Every Veyne in Swich Licour

for John Casteen

Come, spring for summer, blush and simmer thrust
all beaconing to blossom, fulsome, lush
the mulch and lissome burst of it, the fledge,
the shoots unvanquished. Culminate
in song, O sorrowless, O new fruit
and cumulus, the fullness, thirst and slake,
kindle the young of all the recent earth.
This is tongue and muscle, leaf and root
and what begot and whence. Scathe
the landscape, the scorched and salt-sown,
that it yield life as the darkness without form,
touched divine by language, yielded light.
The old undone. The usurper usurped.

The Aged

They sleep in years.
Under the warmth of a single lamp
this epoch passes.
The old music still rings in their ears.

Their stories have widowed them;
there is too much to remember.
The past opens for them
like an unfinished sentence.

There is no night like theirs,
the light the stars yield
as old as anything they could dream,
and slight, at that.

Self-Portrait

Or just some human sleep
—ROBERT FROST

The dead are there, still mulling over
conversations we had started. They return
to the eyelid, to the instant before waking,
but have not said their peace.

This jaw unhinges, these teeth
loosen and rot out.
Behind the crickets I can hear
their ghoulish clatter in the bone-white sink.

There are long drives through mountains
and fields at the edge of a wood, I must know where.
There is falling, wincing,
and sometimes, awkward but steady flight.

And what is there to say
of waking, erect, with the salt
of old love on my lips? What is there
to tell your numb ear, your open mouth?

To a Shade

W. J. C., 1915–2002

I

Knuckle-hard chestnuts suppled in the oven.
On TV, celebrities caroled through confetti snowdrifts.
Even before the timer rang, you reached in
for the pan, bare-handed; shook the lingering
heat from your arthritic fingers. Then
the cracking of shells, steam rising like souls
from the pruned meat. You insisted I take more
than my share: setting them aside as I puffed
to cool my mouth, that taste both sweet and smoldering.
Christ, what a burr-coarse way to miss you.

II

I thought I'd said all
I had to say to you,
but there you are,
hunched in the muddy light
at your workbench,
the scattered brass, cork
and pearl of a tenor sax.
There's the scratch
of your cheek
on mine, your eyes garbled
through safety glasses.
The cool notes of scales
played on piccolo and flute,

oboe, clarinet.
There's the window,
and outside, the willow
practically dripping
all over the backyard.

In Elegy

D. L. L., 1936–2008

Then in February the frost broke,
water ran its whims and jetties where
it could; the lake ice unhinged in schisms
and plurals. Which melt and slide
as plates ride rumors of magma deep
within the world, where we cannot
imagine how slight the shift that steers
us about the rootless earth, so slow
that we never feel how far
we have been ushered, over and across,
our homes as we had left them
but elsewhere; the ground uprooted,
cracks in the firm footing, spills
from the core of the earth into
our little lives. A day and night. And then,
in February too, the cold snap. The ice
again. Another day, hard and fast.

What the Talkers Were Talking

You know what they say
about the body, crying in its thorns.
You've heard it said we do not deserve
the world we have been given—
the tendons and roots and milk of things.
Or maybe no one's said this. Maybe
you've never heard of the dust that falls
and covers us with the sloughed flesh of the dead
in some absurd blessing. —If there even is an us.
Maybe this all sounds like madness,
and you sleep softly though the ocean blasts
beneath you, though the earth turns in the dark.

Of the Tragedies

Do not think of the tragedies,
though they are legion—
oceanic, arriving wave on wave
where the stones lie slick and stunned.
They will return in time, no matter
our prayers or tributes.
There is time enough
for every species of tragedy,
wars that loom their saurian wings
and the miniscule griefs of days.
Do not think of these.
There is still the wine, and the talk
that empties it. There is autumn.
There is music enough
to put quietly to rest
the instrument one never learned to play.

After Strange Gods

To wake among the darkness
of indigo, mineral night,
and to lie there
in the swoon of hours,
the Hunter's slow stalk toward dawn,
is to scent the terrors we have not named.
Pawing and panting at the door—

they were not present in the garden
but lurked in a distant wood
that blackened like a looming squall.
All tongues sing their bleak glory:
Let the cup of night pass from these lips,
there is no sleep that sleeps them off.
There are gods we dare not worship.

Aubade

If sleep, as heard say, is a sea
on which we sail adrift,
the frail craft of self
alee, afar beneath
the rigged mast and spar,
the waters blear and rough—
if this is so, then in sight of shore
there each crest shears itself
of white as sleep shrugs
us from its arms into the swath
of day. Toward dawn,
how we totter there, buoyed
savagely upended,
how we tend toward the shock of sun,
the open wound of light
that silvers there, a sea itself
—sibilant, unbound—
that glitters the staccato surface
and lavishes all in brilliance.

Perchè non parli?

—MICHELANGELO, to his *Moses*

I

It is always this way.

The marble seems to breathe, think.
The glist of light on muscle

could be its first kinetic urge;
he nearly swells with a rage

that moves, instead, the artist:
Why don't you speak?

he said, and scarred
the prophet's stone knee with his hammer.

Moses held the law tight against his chest.

II

I had hoped to peel away
the scab of language

to reveal a rare flesh,
soft as a tongue.

I had hoped for glory, prayer.

I had wanted the right word
to key and pitch itself in me,

to be struck,
like Paul, into belief.

III

What could he have said?
That summer sickens on its own heat,

that silence is the ocean
our words empty into?

Less than life was apprentice work.

It is always this way—

in the pauses gravid with the unsaid,
the sadness after sex.

The Twenty-first Century

Our immortals are dead.
Hymn some other glory—
let the sun shine unsung.
Little we can do
but lay shadows at our feet.
Come into the garden;
the musk of the rose is blown.
Enough, then: praise
pebbles' rattle on the shore.
Sulfur and smoke, praise that.
Read me a book of the dead,
say something in the dark
as if to call forth light.
Little we can do
but ask to live forever.

The New Poetry

for Charles Wright

The new poetry will cough up blood.
Stare, like a dog, at the door
until we shift restlessly in our seats.
It will eat its own young.
Like an ancient star, it will snuff out
beneath its own density
though we wheel ships by its light.
The new poetry will turn wine into wine.
It will not come as a thief:
it will be what is stolen.

Lexicon

lake

Beowulf (Z.) 1584 He..oðer swylc ut of-ferede lað-licu lac.
—*Oxford English Dictionary*

To present an offering. Or, the offering itself.
  A drink of water. A glass held up: an honor, a toast.
  So in rivers and brooks of tide the lake comes calving,
  stressed and breaking across the stony beaches; in light-
  stunned whitecaps it comes in crawls, and recedes, and
  recalls.

To jest, to joust.
  They are not gulls. They are lake-terns, suffering
  and triumphing the strange currents of air above the water,
  and in fetches and darts fishing from just beneath
  the surface. A twitch of eye and they rise, quarry-
  carrying there, there, and there.

A pit or den, a grave.
  Ask the ships, so long surrendered to the shallow,
  but brutal, floor. Ask the foolish boys gone skimming
  the winter skein of snow. Their answers are pockets
  of air bubbled into sheets of ice, silent and crazed.

A wine-vat.
  A camp of bonfires each night, the swell and dispersal
  of laughter across the strand. Here a love, a betrayal,
  the phrases of water over empty bottles.

A large body of water entirely surrounded by land.

Perhaps it was once thought an ocean.

Fine linen.

Crisp whites, snapped as from a line, culled and pinned
across the choppy surface. Threads and strands of vapor
clothed in frost, starched and settled for the long sleep.

A pigment of reddish hue.

There, that trace of sunset addressed across the water,
toward the long horizon, and beyond.

Notes

"Midst of a Burning Fiery Furnace": Daniel 3.

"December 1678, New France": Father Louis Hennepin, the first European to record viewing Niagara Falls; from his travelogue *A New Discovery of a Vast Country in America* (1697).

"River on Fire": Exodus 3:2, Psalms 137:1, Luke 12:49; Adam Again, "River on Fire" (1992).

"Hulett Ore Unloaders": John Mangels, "Hulett job faces 80 years of rust," *Cleveland Plain Dealer*, 31 January 2000.

"'They Wonder at the Star'": From the Latin *ISTI MIRANT STELLA*, inscribed on the Bayeux Tapestry beside a representation of the comet now named for Edmund Halley.

"It Will Be Rain Tonight": William Shakespeare, *Macbeth*.

"On a Portrait by Lucian Freud": *Naked Portrait with Reflection* (1980).

"A Sudden Gust of Wind": Jeff Wall, *A Sudden Gust of Wind* (1993).

"We Who Keep the Mystery": Fyodor Dostoevsky, *The Brothers Karamazov* (1880; translated from the Russian by Richard Pevear and Larissa Volokhonsky, 1990).

"Every Veyne in Swich Licour": Geoffrey Chaucer, *The Canterbury Tales*.

"Self-Portrait": The idiomatic expression I use in the first stanza is most often written as "to speak one's piece." In my family, however, its usage has frequently been understood as I have rendered it here.

"What the Talkers Were Talking": Walt Whitman, "Song of Myself" (1855). The second line is almost entirely lifted from James Wright's poem "Trying to Pray" (1963).

"The Twenty-first Century": Alfred, Lord Tennyson, "Maud" (1855); William Butler Yeats, "The Nineteenth Century and After" (1933).

BOOKS IN THE SERIES

The History of Anonymity
Jennifer Chang

Hardscrabble
Kevin McFadden

Field Folly Snow
Cecily Parks

Boy
Patrick Phillips

Salvinia Molesta
Victoria Chang

Anna, Washing
Ted Genoways

Free Union
John Casteen

Quiver
Susan B. A. Somers-Willett

The Mansion of Happiness
Robin Ekiss

Illustrating the Machine That Makes the World: From J. G. Heck's 1851 Pictorial Archive of Nature and Science
Joshua Poteat

A Wreath of Down and Drops of Blood
Allen Braden

In the World He Created According to His Will
David Caplan

Logorrhea Dementia: A Self-Diagnosis
Kyle G. Dargan

The Lost Boys
Daniel Groves

For the Mountain Laurel
John Casteen

Weather
Dave Lucas